THE TRUTH ABOUT MINISTRY

The Emotional and Spiritual Cost of Leadership

DR. LARRY L. CHARLES II

Author: Dr. Larry L. Charles II
Publisher: Kingdom News Publication Services, LLC.

DISCLAIMER
All the material contained in this book is provided for
educational and informational purposes only. No
responsibility can be taken for any results or outcomes
resulting from the use of this material.

While every attempt has been made to provide
information that is both accurate and effective, the author
does not assume any responsibility for the accuracy or
use/misuse of this information.

Printed in the United States of America.
ISBN 978-1-955127-44-8

DEDICATION

To every weary leader who has stood behind an empty feeling pulpit, preached through pain, and wondered if God still sees — This is for you.

To my wife, my partner in grace, whose love has steadied me for over thirty years, and to our six children and eight grandchildren, who remind me daily that legacy is built in love.

To The Breath of Life Church, a living testimony of God's faithfulness, born in 2009 and still breathing hope into the world.

And to the God who met Elijah under the broom tree, whispered in the cave, and still restores those who are called — This book is my offering.

TABLE OF CONTENTS

INTRODUCTION
THE TRUTH ABOUT MINISTRY

The pulpit is empty.
The spotlight has faded.
And the silence is telling the truth.

Ministry is not always fire from heaven.
Sometimes it's bread in the wilderness.
Sometimes it's a whisper in the cave.
Sometimes it's a prophet curled beneath a broom tree, asking God to let him go.

In *The Truth About Ministry*, Dr. Charles invites weary leaders into the sacred honesty of Elijah's journey — from confrontation to collapse, from burnout to blessing. This is not a manual for performance. It's a map for survival. A guide for those who have poured out everything and wonder if God still sees.

With poetic insight and pastoral depth, Dr. Charles offers wisdom for the soul behind the sermon — the one who stands in the shadows of the pulpit, longing to be restored.

Because the truth about ministry isn't found in the crowd. It's found in the cave and the God who still speaks there.

WHEN THE MANTLE
FEELS HEAVY

I didn't write what began as a sermon that turned into a book from a mountaintop. I wrote it from a broom tree. From the tension of deadlines and decisions. From the weight of leadership; where people depend on you, but you're not sure you have anything left to give. From the grind of a full-time job that doesn't pause for pain. From the pressure of school, the beauty and complexity of family and the sacred responsibility of pastoring a church.

I've had moments where I wanted to quit. I didn't ask God to take my life like Elijah, who I gleaned these insights from. But I did come to Him tired — mentally, emotionally, physically. And He met me there. He gave me rest. He gave me wisdom. He taught me how to pause, how to breathe, how to care for my body and mind without guilt or shame.

This book was born in those moments. Not in triumph, but in truth. Not in perfection, but in process. It's for every leader who's ever felt stretched thin. For every minister who's ever poured out and wondered if there was anything left. For every believer who's ever asked, "Is this what ministry feels like?"

It's not a manual. It's a mirror; a place to reflect, to rest, and to remember that you're not alone. Because the truth about ministry is this: it will stretch you. But it will also reveal God. And if you're willing to walk it — honestly, humbly and with open hands — you'll discover that the mantle you carry is not just a burden. It's a blessing.

CHAPTER 1
The Burnout Behind the Breakthrough

Elijah had just called down fire from heaven. The prophets of Baal were silenced. The people fell on their faces. Revival was breaking out. And then; he ran. Not in celebration, not in victory. He ran in fear – because Jezebel threatened his life. The queen who ruled with intimidation and idolatry sent word: "By this time tomorrow, you'll be dead." And Elijah, fresh off a supernatural victory, collapsed under the weight of a very human threat.

This is one of the most jarring transitions in scripture: from Mount Carmel to the wilderness; from boldness to breakdown; from fire to fatigue. And here's the question for every weary leader: What Jezebels have you on the run? What voices of intimidation, accusation, or exhaustion are chasing you out of your calling? What threats — spoken or unspoken — have caused you to flee emotionally, spiritually, or relationally?

Because Jezebel isn't just a person. She's a pattern. She's the pressure that follows your fire. She's the fear that follows your faith.

This is the truth about ministry: breakthrough doesn't exempt you from burnout. Sometimes, it invites it – because the weight of public victory often crushes private vulnerability. The applause fades, but the expectations remain. The enemy doesn't retreat when you win; he retaliates!

Elijah wasn't weak. He was weary. He wasn't faithless. He was fatigued. He wasn't finished. He was fragile. And God didn't rebuke him. He fed him.

But here's the deeper truth: you don't have disappointment without expectation. Elijah expected transformation — of Jezebel, of Israel, of everything. Instead, he got a death threat.

When our expectations rest in outcomes, disappointment is inevitable. But when our expectations rest in God — His timing, His ways, His whisper — you find peace even when the fire fades. Ministry will always carry expectation. But maturity teaches us where to place it. Not in applause. Not in results, but in God alone.

Scriptural Tie-Ins
- 1Kings 18:36-39 — Fire falls, the people repent
- 1Kings 19:1-4 — Elijah flees Jezebel

- Jeremiah 20:7-9 — The burden of the prophetic fire
- 2Corinthians 4:7-9 — Treasure in jars of clay
- Psalm 62:5 — My expectation is from Him.

Reflection Questions

1. Have you ever felt depleted after a spiritual success? What did that depletion reveal about your expectations?
2. What Jezebels have you on the run in your life today? Are there voices, threats, or pressures that have caused you to flee emotionally, spiritually, or relationally?
3. What does "burnout behind breakthrough" look like in your current season?

Micro-Practice

Take 15 minutes today to write down three recent wins in your life or ministry. Then reflect: What emotional toll did each one take? Invite God into that space; not to fix it, but to sit with you in it.

Daily Decision

Today, I choose to honor my limits without shame. And I choose to rest my expectations in God alone.

Today's Thoughts

_____

_____

_____

_____

CHAPTER 2
Running on Empty

The story is told of a man who didn't feel well. He had done all he knew to do but couldn't put his finger on why he just felt empty. His friends said he should see a doctor. So, the man did just that. He went to the doctor and the doctor drew blood and examined him thoroughly. The doctor looked over the numbers and determined that all was well with the man. He just needed to relax and have a good laugh. So, the doctor prescribed a clown named Grimaldi for him. The doctor said that there was no way for anybody to be in the presence of Grimaldi and leave feeling down and empty.

But the man looked at the doctor and said, with tears streaming down his face, "Grimaldi can't help me, for you see, I am Grimaldi!"

Sadly, that is the condition for many of us as we stand before God's people week after week, month after month, year after year. Oh yeah, you may perform like Grimaldi and wear your mask of perfection, but underneath the mask, you are tired, empty, and frustrated – running on empty.

Elijah was such a man. He didn't just flee; he fled fast. He outran Ahab's chariot. He crossed territory. He left his servant behind, and he kept going.

But the deeper truth is that he wasn't running toward anything — he was running away from everything. He was running away from Jezebel. Away from disappointment. Away from unmet expectations. Away from the weight of ministry; and he was running on empty.

This is the danger of prolonged pouring. You give and give and give until there's nothing left to give. You preach with power but pray with fatigue. You counsel with compassion but collapse in private. You show up for everyone else, but disappear from yourself and those closest to you.

Elijah's legs were moving, but his soul was shutting down. He left his servant in Beersheba, a sign that he was done leading. He sat under a broom tree, a symbol of collapse.

Where is your place of collapse? Do you collapse into a bottle? Into pornography? Into infidelity or unbelief?

This is where Elijah asked to die — a cry of exhaustion, not rebellion. This is the truth about ministry: you can be anointed and empty at the same time. You can be faithful and fatigued. You can be running and still not know where you are going.

But here's the grace: God doesn't just meet us in our momentum. God meets us in our depletion. He sends an angel, bakes bread – notice the bread is on the coals, which means what God prepares takes time. He gives water for the thirst of those depleted. He touches us again. God declares the journey is too great. God doesn't demand more when you have nothing left. He provides.

Scriptural Tie-Ins

- 1Kings 19:3-7 — Elijah flees, leaves servant, collapses.
- Psalm 42:5 — Why are you cast down O my soul?
- Matthew 11:28-30 — Come unto me all that are heavy laden...
- Isaiah 40:28-31 — Strength for the weary

Reflection Questions

1. What signs show up in your life when you're running on empty?
2. Have you ever left someone behind emotionally or relationally during a season of exhaustion?
3. What does your "broom tree" look like; a place of collapse, confession or quiet?
4. What would it look like to let God feed you instead of fix you?

Micro-Practice
Take ten minutes to sit in silence. No phone. No agenda. No performance. Just breathe and say, "God, I'm tired and I trust You to meet me here."

Daily Decision
Today, I choose to stop running and start receiving.

Today's Thoughts

_____

_____

_____

_____

_____

_____

_____

_____

_____

_____

_____

_____

_____

_____

_____

_____

_____

_____

_____

_____

CHAPTER 3
Who We Leave in Beersheba

Elijah didn't just run; he detached himself. He left his servant in Beersheba without explanation, without farewell — just distance. And that detail matters. Because Beersheba wasn't just any town; it was the southernmost edge of the territory, the boundary line, the last stop before the wilderness. To leave someone in Beersheba was to leave them on the edge of what was known - to say, "I'm going beyond where you can follow." To walk away from companionship, covering, and community into isolation.

When leaders are overwhelmed, we often isolate – not out of pride, but out of pain. We leave people on the edge of our pain. We stop returning phone calls. We cancel meetings. We emotionally withdraw. It's not because we don't love the people we leave behind; it's that we don't know how to let them into our pain, and we don't want to seem weak, inept, or inadequate.

Who have you left in Beersheba? People who were loyal. People who were assigned. People who were willing to walk with you.

Somehow, pain has a way of convincing us that we're better off alone – that no one understands, that no one can assist you in carrying the weight of emptiness.

This is the truth about ministry, but it's not just ministry – because you can feel empty in all kinds of walks of life: marriage, maternity and paternity — emptiness knows no bounds.

There is some hope for those of us that may be feeling empty right now, and we learn it from Elijah: God still came – not to scold him for leaving his servant, but to remind him, "You are not alone. You were never meant to carry this alone."

Scriptural Tie-Ins
- 1 Kings 19:3-4 – Elijah in the wilderness wanting to die.
- Ecclesiastes 4:9-10 – Companionship and shared support
- 2 Timothy 2:13 – Faithful despite failure.

Reflection Questions
1. Who have you left in Beersheba emotionally, relationally, spiritually?

2. Beersheba was the southernmost edge of the territory. Who have you left on the edge of what's familiar, unable to follow you into your pain?
3. What fears or pressures cause you to isolate yourself from those assigned to walk with you?
4. How do you respond when you feel overwhelmed?
5. What relationships has God placed in your life to help carry the weight of ministry? Have you honored or distanced them?

Micro-practice

Today, write the name of someone or something you've had to leave in your Beersheba. Then write this prayer: "God, I trust you with what I had to release. Heal what I can't carry."

Daily Decision

Today, I choose to release without regret. I will trust God with what I had to leave behind.

Today's Thoughts

_____

_____

_____

_____

_____

_____

CHAPTER 4
The Broom Tree Moment
a Place of Collapse

Elijah didn't collapse in rebellion. He collapsed in exhaustion. He collapsed in isolation. He found a place he could remove his mask of perfection and strength. He sat under a broom tree alone, depleted, undone, and prayed the prayer no prophet wants to admit: "Lord, take my life."

This wasn't a crisis of calling. It was a crisis of capacity. He was anointed but empty. He had seen the power of God, but he was empty. He had spoken truth to power, but he was empty. He had run too far and poured out too much. He had carried too many expectations, and now he had nothing left.

The broom tree wasn't a place of disgrace; it was a place of grace. God didn't bring rebuke to Elijah under his broom tree. God didn't demand more. He didn't quote Elijah's resume or remind him of Mount Carmel. God sent an angel. God baked bread. God gave him water. God touched him twice, and God let him sleep.

What I see in heaven's interaction with the prophet is that God restores in stages, not all at once – not in a rush, but according to timing, maturity, capacity, and relationship. Jesus tells the disciples in John 16:12 that "there are things I have to tell you that you are not able to bear now." This was a sign that it was not time, and they were not mature enough nor had the capacity to receive what God had for them at that moment.

God knows what you're ready for. God knows what you can carry. God knows when to whisper and when to wait. And when God feeds you, God doesn't use a microwave. God prepared a meal for the prophet on coals. God does the same in our lives as well. He doesn't prepare what He has for us in a microwave; he prepares on the coals. This is slow, intentional, and personal preparation. This isn't fast food; it is soul food.

God provides for the hunger and thirst not just of the body but of the soul. I am reminded of what He did for David, leading beside the still waters and restoring his soul.

This is the truth about ministry: collapse is not failure. It's often the beginning of restoration.

The broom tree is where God reminds us, "I see you." Not as a prophet, not as a performer, but as a person – as one of His sheep in need of the shepherd's care. Sometimes the most spiritual thing we can do is rest. This is not retreat. This is not resignation. This is rest. You don't have to feel guilty about needing to rest. Please take the time to rest. Because God doesn't just restore your strength; He restores your soul!

Scriptural Tie-Ins
- Psalm 147:3 — He heals the brokenhearted and binds up their wounds.
- Philippians 1:6 — God completes the work He begins.
- Isaiah 28:10 — Healing and growth often come line upon line, precept upon precept.

Reflection Questions
1. What does your broom tree moment look like?
2. In what ways has God restored you in stages; through timing, maturity, capacity and relationship?
3. What microwave expectations have you carried into your healing journey? How might God be inviting you to trust His slower, coal-fired process?
4. How has God provided for both your hunger and your thirst— not just physically, but spiritually and emotionally?
5. What would it look like to receive rest as a spiritual discipline, not a sign of failure?

Micro-Practice

Find a quiet space and rest; no agenda, no productivity. Let this be a sacred space.

Daily Decision

I choose to honor my limits and receive rest as holy.

Today's Thoughts

_____
_____
_____
_____
_____
_____
_____
_____
_____
_____
_____
_____
_____
_____
_____
_____
_____
_____
_____

CHAPTER 5
Another Touch

Elijah was touched once, and it wasn't enough. So, God touched him again.

We all need another touch just like we need another chance. Because healing doesn't always happen in a single moment. Sometimes it comes in layers. Sometimes it takes another touch. The first touch gave Elijah rest; the second touch gave him strength. The first met the need of his body; the second met the needs of his soul.

This is the truth about ministry: God doesn't rush restoration. He repeats it. He knows that one nap won't fix years of fatigue. God knows one meal won't undo months of depletion. One prayer won't heal a lifetime of pressure. So, God comes again. He sends the angel again. He prepares bread again. He touches again.

We could fast-forward to the New Testament and see Jesus in Mark 8:22-25 engaging a blind man who he had to touch twice. Not everything with God is instantaneous; sometimes it comes in stages.

Could it be that God is doing a multiple-stage work in your life right now? The word of the Lord came unto Jonah a second time, revealing that God met the prophet right where he was and gave him another chance. I'm so glad that we serve a God of another chance – because I used my second chance up a long time ago!

Our Bible declares that the just fall down seven times and rise up again (Prov.24:16). You may be down right now, but God says it's time to get up; He's giving you another chance with another touch.

Scriptural Tie-Ins
- 1 Kings 19:5-7 – Divine sustenance
- Mark 8:22-25 – Gradual restoration
- Proverbs 24:16 – Resilience in failure

Reflection Questions
1. Have you ever felt disappointed that one spiritual moment didn't fix everything?
2. What areas of your life might be in need of another touch; not because God failed but because healing takes time?
3. How has God revealed himself to you in stages?
4. What expectations have you placed on your own healing that may need to be surrendered to God's pace?

Micro-Practice

Ask God for another touch. It will not be out of desperation, but out of trust. Say aloud: "God, I receive your layered healing. I'm not rushing. I'm resting."

Daily Decision

Today, I choose to trust the process. Healing may take time, but God is faithful to finish what He started.

Today's Thoughts

_____
_____
_____
_____
_____
_____
_____
_____
_____
_____
_____
_____
_____
_____
_____
_____
_____

CHAPTER 6
The Journey Is Too
Great for You

What do you do when God reminds you that you are not enough by yourself?

Elijah had rested. He had eaten. He had been touched twice, and still he wasn't ready.

Restoration isn't just about recovery. It's about readiness.

Elijah wasn't ready for the next leg of the journey, so God said plainly: "The journey is too great for you." Not as a rebuke, but as a release. Elijah must have been so relieved to learn that he was given permission to be imperfect and not required to be superhuman.

The truth is, Elijah was exhausted, fearful and hiding – yet God still recommissioned him. Elijah's weakness didn't cancel his calling; it actually attracted God's strength. We hear God say to a great Apostle of the New Testament: "My grace is sufficient for you, that in times of weakness, my strength is made perfect." We don't experience the perfect strength of God until we acknowledge our imperfect weakness in God.

This is the truth about ministry: God doesn't expect you to carry what He hasn't equipped you to endure. He acknowledges your limits. He honors your humanity. God provides for your weakness. God doesn't just give you strength without a strategy. He fed Elijah, not to finish the race, but to survive the next stretch. God didn't say, "You should be stronger." God says, "Eat again. Rest again. The journey is long."

God knows what's ahead. God knows you can't get there on adrenaline alone. So, God provides bread. Water. Rest. Because the journey is too great for you, but not too great for the God who walks with you.

Scriptural Tie-Ins
- 1Kings 19:7-8 — The journey is too great for you.
- 2Corinthians 12:9 — My grace is sufficient.
- Psalm 103:14 — He knows our frame.
- Isaiah 40:29 — He gives power to the faint.

Reflection Questions
1. What journey are you currently on that feels too great for you?

2. How do you respond when God acknowledges your limits; do you resist or receive?
3. What provision has God given you for the next stretch of your journey? Have you received it fully?
4. In what ways have you tried to push forward on adrenaline instead of grace?
5. What would it look like to walk with God at the pace of provision, not pressure?

Micro-Practice

Today, name the journey you're on. Write it down. Then write this beneath it: "This journey is too great for me; but not too great for God."

Daily Decision

Today, I choose to walk with God, not ahead of Him. I will not shame my limits. I will trust His provision.

Today's Thoughts

_____

_____

_____

_____

_____

_____

_____

_____

_____

_____

CHAPTER 7
The Whisper Over the Wind

Elijah stood on the mountain, waiting for God to speak. He had seen fire before, he had called it down. He had watched it consume the altar and silence the prophets of Baal. But this time, the fire wasn't God. Neither was the wind. Neither was the earthquake. God wasn't in the spectacle – God was in the whisper.

The truth about ministry: God doesn't always speak through the grand and the glorious; sometimes God speaks through presence. Not in the noise, but in the nuance. Now, to hear the whisper requires proximity. It demands stillness. It invites intimacy.

And here's the deeper truth: God doesn't always repeat how He revealed Himself before. He's not bound to fire. He's not limited to wind. He's not confined to earthquakes. God is not in a box. God is in a relationship.

And the whisper? It's not weak — it's weighty. It's the kind of voice that doesn't need volume to carry authority. It's the kind of presence that doesn't need spectacle to be sacred.

Just ask Peter. He was in the middle of a storm — waves crashing, wind howling — yet he heard Jesus say, "Come." One word carried on the wind, and Peter heard it and stepped out. Because when Jesus speaks, even the wind becomes a messenger. Even the storm becomes a sanctuary. That which had the potential to cause others to stress and be filled with anxiety Peter turned into an opportunity to be with Jesus.

What are you calling your current storm? Is it a sanctuary or a stress stadium? Elijah had to learn that the God who sent fire on Carmel was the same God who whispered on Horeb. Same God. Different expression; deeper revelation.

Scriptural Tie-Ins
- 1Kings 19:11-13 — God's not in the wind or fire, but in a whisper.
- Psalm 46:10 — Be still and know.
- John 10:27 — My sheep hear my voice.
- Isaiah 30:21 — Your ears shall hear a word behind you.

Reflection Questions
1. Have you ever expected God to speak through spectacle only to find Him in silence?

2. What does the whisper of God sound like in your life; how do you recognize it?
3. How has God shifted the way he speaks to you over time?
4. What distractions or noise might be keeping you from hearing the whisper?
5. What would it look like to cultivate stillness as a spiritual discipline?

Micro-Practice
Today, spend 10 minutes in silence. No requests. No agenda. Just listen. Write down anything you sense, feel, or hear in the quiet.

Daily Choice
Today, I choose to lean into the whisper. I will not chase spectacle; I will seek presence.

Today's Thoughts

_____

_____

_____

_____

_____

_____

_____

_____

_____

_____

CHAPTER 8
The Cave and the Commission

Elijah didn't just collapse; he crawled into a cave. Not to rest, and not to retreat, but to receive. He had seen the fire and he had seen the angel, but he wasn't ready to reemerge.

Sometimes, even after God speaks, we stay hidden — not out of rebellion, but out of residue. The residue of fear. The residue of fatigue. The residue of perceived failure.

And this isn't the first time we've heard of something like this from a leader. Saul hid among the baggage after being anointed to be king. He had heard the voice. He had received the oil. He had been chosen, and still, he hid.

We have to know that calling doesn't cancel insecurity. Anointing doesn't erase anxiety. Sometimes, the weight of what God says feels heavier than the silence that came before.

This is the truth about ministry: God meets you in the cave — not to expose you, but to recommission you. He listened to Elijah's lament without interruption. Have you ever just needed somebody to listen to you without interruption and without judgment? God just let Elijah pout it all out, then He spoke into the fog of frustration — the truth about the remnant that remained. Then God gave him an assignment: go back and anoint kings, and choose Elisha as your successor.

What God was revealing was that the cave was not the end. The cave was the place between the collapse and the calling.

God doesn't need you to be perfect to recommission you; He just needs you to be honest.

Many times, in the church today, we call on our leaders to be holy but not honest. The cave is where God says, "I still have work for you. I still trust you. I still see you."

So, if you're in a cave, don't rush out. But don't stay forever either. The whisper leads to the commission, and the commission leads to legacy. Get up — you're closer than you think!

Scriptural Tie-Ins
- 1Kings 19:9-16 — Elijah in the cave, recommissioned
- Psalm 142:1-7 — A prayer from the cave

- Jonah 2:1-10 — A recommissioning from the belly
- John 21:15-17 — Peter recommissioned after denial

Reflection Questions

1. What does your cave look like emotionally, spiritually, or relationally?
2. What residue are you carrying that makes it hard to reemerge?
3. How has God met you in hidden places not with condemnation, but with compassion?
4. What assignment has God placed before you, even while you were still healing?
5. What would it look like to say "yes" to God's commission from a place of honesty, not perfection?

Micro-Practice

Today, write a short prayer from your cave. Name what you're feeling. Then ask God, "What are you calling me to next?"

Daily Decision

Today, I choose to listen from the cave. I will not confuse hiding with healing. I am still called.

Today's Thoughts

_____

_____

_____

CHAPTER 9
The Mantle and the Movement

Elijah didn't leave the cave with fireworks. He left with a mantle. The mantle was a prophet's outer garment, often a cloak or robe, but its meaning went far beyond mere fabric. It's a symbol of calling, continuity, and divine authority. Let's take a closer look at the mantle:

- **Identity and Office**: The mantle marked Elijah as a prophet of God. It was a visible sign of his role, much like a crown for a king or a priestly ephod.
- To wear the mantle was to carry the identity of one set apart.
- **Authority and Anointing**: When Elijah cast his mantle on Elisha (1Kings 19:19), it wasn't just clothing; it was a transfer of spiritual authority.
- The mantle symbolized the weight of God's anointing, the responsibility to speak His word, and the authority to act in His name.
- **Continuity and Legacy**: The mantle connected generations. Elijah's mantle didn't die with him; it was picked up by Elisha (2Kings 2:13-14).

- It represented the ongoing work of God, reminding us that ministry is bigger than one person's lifetime.
- **Burden and Blessing**: The mantle was heavy — not physically, but spiritually. It carried the burden of obedience, the cost of leadership, and the weight of responsibility.
- Yet it was also a blessing, a tangible reminder that God equips those He calls.

Elijah left with his mantle because restoration isn't just about recovery; it's about responsibility. God didn't just heal Elijah – He handed him a next step. A next generation. A movement. "Go and find Elisha."

This is the truth about ministry: healing always leads to handling off. Not because you're done, but because you're not meant to do it alone. The mantle wasn't just a symbol; it was a strategy. It was God saying, "I'm building something beyond you."

And Elijah obeyed. He threw the mantle on Elisha. No speech. No ceremony. Just a gesture. But that gesture carried weight – because mantles don't just fall. They're passed.

And here's the deeper truth: legacy begins when you stop hoarding your healing and start sharing your journey. Elijah didn't wait until he felt strong; he moved while still tender. He mentored while still healing. He led while still listening. Because movements don't need perfect leaders – they need honest ones.

Mantles don't require applause. They require obedience.

Who are you investing in for the next generation? Success is not successful without a successor.

Scriptural Tie-Ins

- 1Kings 19:19-21 — Elijah finds Elisha and throws his mantle.
- 2Kings 2:13-14 — Elisha picks up the mantle.
- Deuteronomy 34:9 — Moses lays hands on Joshua.
- John 21:17 — Jesus recommissions Peter: "Feed my sheep."

Reflection Questions

1. What mantle has God placed in your hands; not just for you, but for someone coming after you?
2. How do you respond to the call to mentor, equip, or release others while still healing?
3. What fears or insecurities might keep you from passing the mantle?
4. Who is your Elisha? Who is the someone God has placed near you to walk with, pour into and prepare?
5. What would it look like to lead from a place of honesty, not arrival?

Micro-Practice

Today, identify one person you can encourage, mentor, or equip. Send a message, make a call or pray intentionally for them. Say aloud: "God, help me pass what you've placed in me."

Daily Decision

Today, I choose to pass the mantle. I will not wait for perfection. I will move with purpose.

Today's Thoughts

_____

_____

_____

_____

_____

_____

_____

_____

_____

_____

_____

_____

_____

_____

_____

_____

CHAPTER 10
The Truth About Ministry

Well, we have come to the end of our journey together with Elijah, which becomes a mirror for every leader who's ever felt called, crushed, and carried. Ministry is not just fire on the mountain. It's fatigue under the broom tree. It's whispers in the wind. It's caves and commissions. It's mantles and movements.

The truth about ministry is that it's the tension between calling and collapse. It's the space between the anointing and the anxiety — between public power and private pain.

The truth about ministry is this: you can be chosen and still feel crushed. You can be anointed and still want to hide. Just ask Elijah. Just ask Saul. Just ask Peter.

You can hear the voice of God and still retreat into silence. You can receive the mantle and still wrestle with your mind. You can lead a movement and still need another touch.

And God? God is not surprised. God is not disappointed. God is not boxed in by your breakdown. He will meet you where you are. He will minister to you in stages. He feeds slowly. He whispers gently. He recommissions you honestly — because ministry is not about being impressive; it's about being intimate. It's not about being strong; it's about being surrendered.

The truth about ministry is that it will stretch you. It will break you. It will empty you — but it will also reveal God. Not just in the fire, but in the whisper. Not just in the crowd, but also in the cave. And if you're willing to walk it — not perfectly, but honestly — you'll find that the mantle you carry is not just for you. It's for the movement God is building through you.

Scriptural Tie-Ins
- 1Kings 19 (entire chapter)
- 2Corinthians 4:7-9 — Treasure in jars of clay
- John 21:15-17 — Peter recommissioned after denial
- Romans 11:29 — The gifts and calling of God are irrevocable.

Reflection Questions
1. What has this journey through Elijah's story revealed about your own ministry experience?
2. Where have you felt the tension between calling and collapse?

3. How has God met you in stillness?
4. What part of your story might be a mantle for someone else's movement?
5. What does it mean for you to walk in ministry — not perfectly, but honestly?

Micro-Practice
Today, write a brief letter to yourself as a minister. Affirm your calling. Acknowledge your pain and invite God to continue the work He started.

Daily Decision
Today, I choose to walk in the truth about ministry. I am called. I am human. I am held.

Today's Thoughts

_____

_____

_____

_____

_____

_____

_____

_____

_____

_____

_____

_____

Closing Benediction
For the Wounded and the Willing

May you never confuse exhaustion with failure.
May you never mistake silence for absence.
May you never believe that your limits disqualify
your calling.

You are not alone. You are not forgotten. You are not
finished.

May the God who met Elijah under the broom tree
meet you in your weariness. May He feed you
slowly, speak to you gently, and restore you layer by
layer.

May you hear the whisper above the wind. May you
receive His touch again and again. May you rest
without guilt, lead without pretending and walk
without rushing. May you find your cave to be a
classroom, your mantle to be a movement, and your
ministry to be a mirror of grace.

Now go in the strength of the One who knows your
frame, honors your journey, and walks with you
every step of the way.

Amen

www.ingramcontent.com/pod-product-compliance
Lightning Source LLC
Chambersburg PA
CBHW072036060426
42449CB00010BA/2297